## ***Praise Abo***

It is always said, "that a gooc grandmother once said, "Show ..., I'll show you your future." Those words are so true. Marilyn Evans is that friend. She's the epitome of a best friend, a beautiful person, but more than that a great contributor to her community. Her ability to guide people through any challenge is unparalleled. Marilyn has a gift from God. She has the gift to inspire.

-Cavanaugh M.

I am proud of the woman Mi Mi has become. I have stood by and witnessed her grow and blossom into the Mighty Woman of God she is today. I am blessed to call her my Big Sister. Can't wait for the next chapter! I love you!!

-Tajana B.

As I think about my sister, yes, my sister. We may not be blood sisters—but as in the Bible—we are all sisters and brothers in Christ. As I observe you often, in my opinion, you remind me in part of Proverbs 31:10, "Who can find a virtuous woman"; because she is hard working, she is good, she is trustworthy, she plans wisely, and she is her brother's and sister's keeper. She is always fighting, not for herself, but for others to have a brighter and more successful outcome than she had. She has grown so from the first time that I saw her, and she fully saw me (with her enlarged eyes ♡). She's an individual that is striving to do the right thing and right unto others. As you may be aware in the reading, I refer to she... she is:

M—Motivated

A—Ambitious

R—Relentless

I—Independent

L—Loved

Y— Youthful

N-Nurturing...

-Sheyann C.

My Aunt Marilyn is a very caring and a hardworking person. She is very dedicated in what she does. She is also a big motivational speaker. I see her as a leader. She has had a big impact on my life since I was a little kid, and she has pushed me through whatever life throws at me and she has always had my back. I wouldn't be the man I am today if it wasn't for you. Thanks.

-Dee R.

# When The Little Girl Is Healed, The Woman Will Show Up

---

Marilyn Evans

**When The Little Girl Is Healed,**
**The Woman Will Show Up**
A Memoir

A guide for those affected by depression, sexual assault, molestation, and unresolved anger. Trust the process to healing, peace, and forgiveness.

Marilyn Evans

**Copyright**

When The Little Girl Is Healed, The Woman Will Show Up
A Memoir
Copyright 2021 by Marilyn Evans

All rights reserved. No part of this book may be reproduced or transmitted in any form or by any means without written permission from the author.

ISBN 978-1-5323-2079-8
Printed in USA by

Scriptures marked NLT are taken from the HOLY BIBLE, New Living Translation (NLT). *Holy Bible*, New Living Translation, copyright © 1996, 2004, 2015 by Tyndale House Foundation. Used by permission of Tyndale House Publishers, Inc., Carol Stream, Illinois 60188. All rights reserved. Scripture quoted by permission.
Scriptures marked NIV are taken from the New International Version (NIV). Scripture taken from The Holy Bible, New International Version®, NIV® Copyright ©1973, 1978, 1984, 2011 by Biblica, Inc.® Used by permission. All rights reserved worldwide. Scripture quoted by permission.
Scriptures marked NKJV are taken from the New King James Version (NKJV). Scripture taken from the New King James Version®. Copyright © 1982 by Thomas Nelson. Used by permission. All rights reserved. Scripture quoted by permission.
Scriptures marked KJV are taken from the King James Version (KJV). King James Version. Public Domain.
Scriptures marked ESV are taken from the English Standard Version (ESV). The Holy Bible, English Standard Version. ESV® Text Edition: 2016. Copyright © 2001 by Crossway Bibles, a publishing ministry of Good News Publishers. Scripture quoted by permission.

# Dedication

My book is dedicated to...

Anybody who has battled depression to the point where you feel like you do not want to live any longer.

Anyone who has been so angry you wanted to hurt someone or hurt yourself.

Anyone whose soul is crying out so much that you become numb to the mental, spiritual, and physical pain.

I know it is difficult. I have experienced every one of these emotions and the pain. I pray that while reading my book God will speak to your spirit and that you are healed in Jesus' name because if He did it for me, He can do it for you.

# Table of Contents

# Acknowledgments

First and foremost, I would like to thank and acknowledge God for answering my prayer and allowing me to walk in my purpose that He designed just for me. With prayer and fasting and seeking God's guidance, I was able to write this book. From depression, anger, and pain, I was able to birth my purpose and write this book, *When the Little Girl Is Healed, The Woman Will Show Up.*

But most of all I would like to thank my family and friends. I also would like to thank my dear friends, Tajana Bagley and Candace B. Woods for inspiration and faith in me during the process of writing my book.

Last but not least, I would like to thank my mom, Mary Goldsby and my dad, the late Eddie Goldsby. I am so grateful, humble, thankful, and truly blessed to have them as my parents. I am so happy for my mom and so proud that she has been sober for three years. I love you Momma. I love you, sisters, and brother and all my nieces and nephews and family and friends that have been there with me through this journey called life.

Thank you, Lord, for turning my pain into my purpose. If You would have never died on the cross for me, I would have never been here. Thank you.

Love, Marilyn

## Foreword
## Pain for Purpose

*Candace B. Woods*

*When The Little Girl is Healed, The Woman Will Show Up*, is the dynamic, transparent journey of a woman I have grown to deeply admire and that I now call friend. I had the pleasure of coaching Marilyn as she courageously embarked upon her journey toward purpose. Marilyn did not take this opportunity to share her story lightly. She knew that somehow the abuse, neglect, and her pain was not unnecessary, and her journey of healing and restoration would touch the heart of those who need it the most.

From the moment we began working on this book, Marilyn made it clear that she wanted and needed to allow herself to be vulnerable. She knew that this part of her journey would solidify her healing in a major way. She wants others who can relate to her story to know that there is help for them and that they too, can heal and learn how to use their pain for purpose.

One of my favorite quotes was stated by the late Steve Job, cofounder of Apple, Inc. He said "If you are working on something exciting you really care about, you don't have to be pushed. The vision pulls you." If I could think of anyone who reflects the thoughts of Mr. Jobs when he wrote this quote, it would be Marilyn Evans. Marilyn was clear from the beginning of this process about her vision for her book. Her journey of birthing this book was not easily. There were many tears and moments when she would call and say, "Coach, today was rough, but I will not quit. She was determined to press her way through fear, through depression, and moments of doubt. She knew she could not quit. She allowed the vision God placed in her heart, to pull her through.

It is my hearts prayer that every reader will be inspired by Marilyn's story to do the work necessary to ensure that the little girl or little boy within them is healed so that they too can lead and live a life that is purposeful and meaningful.

# Introduction

I took my life back when God said, *"I am going to turn your pain into your purpose. Marilyn, your voice will be heard. Your tears will be tears of joy and not pain. You will overcome the physical and mental abuse."*

Several years ago, I said enough is enough I will no longer be in a parent/ child role reversal because of my mom's drinking and neglect. I had to forgive myself and forgive my mom for not protecting me from this preparator she called her friend who molested me. Because of the poor supervision and alcoholism from my mom, I and my siblings experienced so much too soon. I had sex at an early age—looking for a love in all the wrong men. Also, I was a parent to my sisters while I was a child myself. I experienced being bullied and was even touched by a someone I didn't know. My sister became pregnant at 16 and my youngest sister losing her way in the world and going to prison.

I felt like I lost everything at age 16 when Daddy died. A daddy's love is unbreakable and forever. He was my protector and after he died, I was left in this world to take care of and protect myself. Although I did not realize it then, the heavenly Father, my God, was not only taking care of me but also protecting me.

God delivered me from the generational curses like childhood pregnancy, alcoholism, gambling, and poverty. He also delivered me from those statistical "norms" for children raised in the projects. I tell my nephews and nieces all the time that "you don't have to be a product of your environment". God healed me from anger, depression, and suicidal thoughts. I have had breakthroughs with my mom and peace has come over me. God allowed me to birth a miracle, my first published book, *When The Little Girl is Healed, The Woman Will Show Up.*

You will learn from reading my book how I healed from molestation and how I learned to forgive which gave me the peace I had been seeking. And you can too. (I have included some resources at the back of the book that I hope will be helpful to you and/or someone you know.)

I want you to know that you can heal from the inside out from sexual assault. God can release you from that spirit of depression, anger, and suicidal thoughts. He will show you how to heal physically, mentally, and spiritually but you have to be willing to give it to God and watch the blessings overflow in your life. Watch God give you peace, healing, and the understanding you need when you give Him your hurt and your pain. When you do this, you will learn how to make your faith stronger and not to lean on our own understanding and how to distinguish between God's voice and the enemy's voice.

I have learned that sometimes, we stand in our way, we are our own worst critic, and we hold ourselves back unknowingly. I encourage you to listen with your heart and not our emotions.

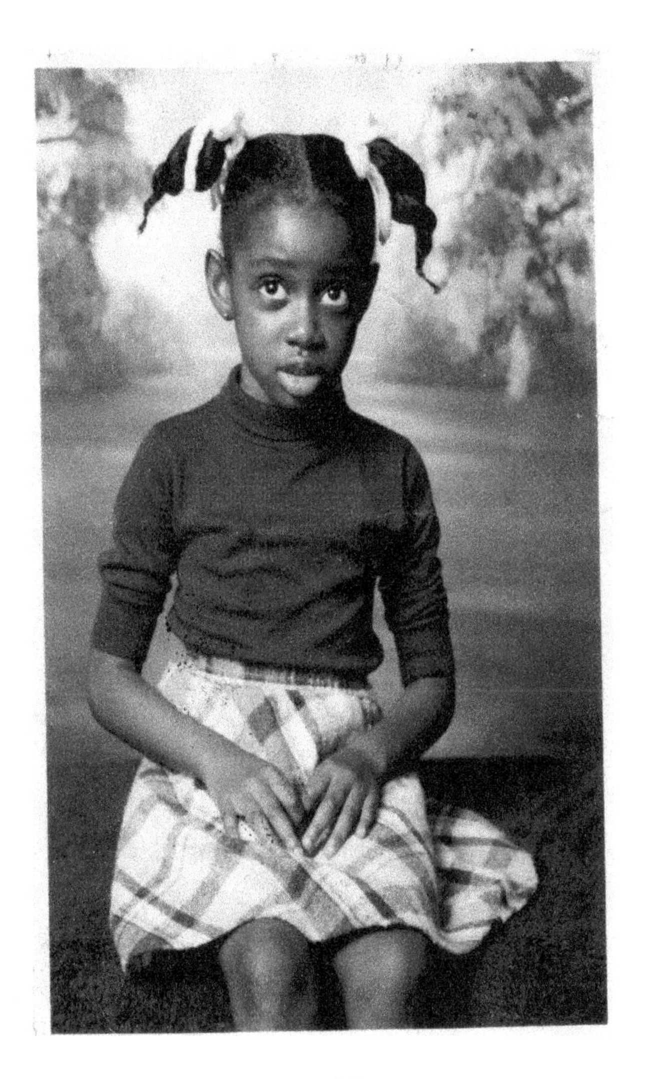

## Just The 2 Of Us

I am the oldest child of my mom. Daddy had a total of seven children. He had one son and a daughter by his first wife and then, there is a sister 10 years older than me by another woman. Mom and Dad have four children together.

Before there were four children, it was just me. We moved to the projects, Riverside Heights, right outside Maxwell Air Force Base in Montgomery,

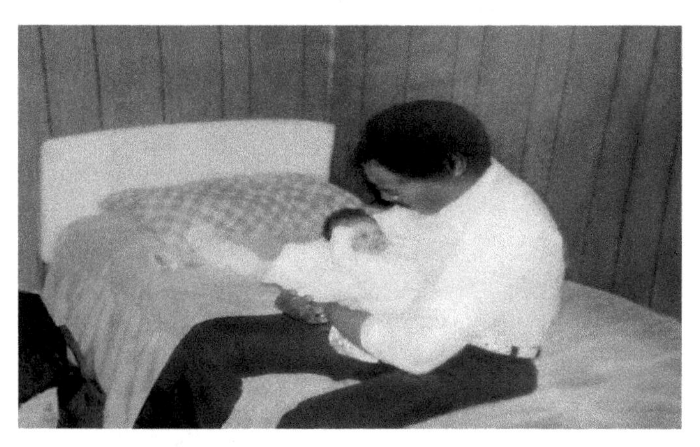

***Before there were four children, it was just me.***

Alabama, when I was three years old. Before moving there, we lived in an old house on Holcombe Street. It wasn't too far from our new home. When I became grown, I would drive by that old house. It looked like a big mansion. Mama said we lived with this lady who thought I was her baby.

Momma met Daddy when she was 19 years old. Daddy was 22 years Momma's senior, but you could not tell because he never treated her any different. He treated her as his wife, and he loved her. Momma had me when she was 22.

It was just me for three years, then my sister, Hester, was born. Later, we got a dog. His name was Butch. He was a pit bull with a white stripe under his neck. We lived in a two-bedroom apartment. In my room, I had a let-out couch, and my sister had a baby bed that had a few poles missing out of it which is how she would escape; she was my partner in crime. Momma said I treated her like she was my doll and baby.

I attended Head Start at the Nellie Burge Community Center. I remember these two girls named Keke and Mimi—they had this beautiful mother that worked there— we became friends. We remained friends even after high school.

For elementary school, we attended McMillan Elementary. Daddy would walk me to school or drive me. We had this green four-door Datsun. In kindergarten, I had a teacher who was very tall but on my first day I didn't care about any of that. The thought of my Daddy leaving me was not working for me... You are not going to leave me with this lady. I was crying so hard that she took me and gave me a sucker and Daddy sneaked out while my attention was on getting the sucker. I was ok after that.

Then, I had a teacher in 2nd grade that looked like an Indian. She liked Daddy. She would always be twisting when she saw him. The only thing I did not like about her was if you didn't know an arithmetic answer to the problems you were given, she would pop you with a ruler on your knuckles. I got plenty. I didn't like math at all—still don't. I also had a teacher in 3rd grade that had gray hair that used to poked from under her wig. She liked Daddy, also.

I always had friends and had them for a long time. Most of my friends had both parents in the home. I always had that family foundation in my life. I guess that's why I am so strong on family as my foundation.

***I always had that family foundation in my life.***

# Innocent

I enjoyed playing with the neighborhood kids. I was a tomboy who is what they called it back then. I was straight up and down, no breasts and no butt just long hair and big eyes. I remember putting tissue in my bra sometimes to make me look like I had breasts. Of course, Momma found out and I had to stop.

I loved playing kickball and baseball with the boys in the neighborhood. Daddy walked back and forth to the door to check on me to make sure they were not too rough or trying anything. One time though, I caught a ball in the eye and had to go in the house. Daddy was fussing and I was mad and crying because I wanted to stay outside and play.

I tried skating until I fell into a dip in the yard that I did not see. It knocked the breath out of me. When I got up, I couldn't breathe. I never got on two skates again. After that, I skated with one shoe and one skate. It looked weird but it worked for me.

I never rode a bike. We could not afford one and the fear of falling off when I got older, just was not for me. As children at Christmas, the fire department and the police department would bring us Christmas presents.

As I got older, I realized we were poor, but we were happy. We always had food. We got food stamps and the block cheese. It made great grilled cheese sandwiches. Daddy used to make the best grilled cheese. Daddy could cook well for a man. He would make crackling bread, fried tomatoes, fried okra, and fried corn off the cob. (I did not like shelling peas, and I didn't like cleaning corn off the cob.) We always had a hot meal.

When Momma was working, Daddy cooked and when Daddy was working, Momma would cook. They never worked at the same time because somebody had to be home with us.

I used to love the 1st and the 3rd of the month because Daddy got an SSI check on the 1st and the big check, his Social Security, on the 3rd. He got one for us, too. Those would be really the only times we would go outside our neighborhood. We would drive to Fairview Avenue to get some Church's chicken or something. Fairview Avenue was a busy street that had all sorts of fast-food restaurants and grocery and clothing stores. If you wanted to find anything, you could find it on Fairview. Going to Fairview Avenue was certainly a treat for us and one that we really looked forward to.

Momma always had a kind soul. She would give her last. When she cooked and she was working, she would always over cook and take food to people she worked with it. She feeds the homeless people in the neighborhood she lives in now. She even feeds people that do work around her house when she doesn't have the money to pay them.

My mom is a short and feisty lady. She didn't back down from nobody, man, or woman. I hated when Momma would drink though. When she got mad and she was drinking, she would fold that bottom lip up. Oh yeah, you were going to get cussed out from A-Z and she going to make you get off of her porch. But the next day whomever she cussed out the day before, they would be sitting outside talking like nothing had happened. I used to tell her she was going to lose friends like that because I wouldn't keep coming around for that kind of abuse. She would just laugh, or she would say stay out of my business. (I see a lot of Momma in my sisters, Hester, and Red.)

When my mom drank, she would play music very loud. Daddy didn't like that. Most of the time, he would take her albums and throw them out the front door.

She also had this habit when she would drink—she would walk the neighborhood. I used to be so scared for my Momma. One night, she went across to this lady's house she knew and there was a man over there. He slapped my Momma and blood came from her nose. Well, Momma came home, and Daddy saw Momma's nose. All I know is Daddy said do not let nobody in while he was gone. Daddy and Momma went back across that street and Daddy had his gun. When they came back, I heard Daddy say, "Don't nobody put your hands on my wife." Knowing Daddy, I am sure it did not go that smoothly, but that problem was handled.

One thing about my daddy, Eddie, he loved his girls, and his wife and Daddy did not care who you were or who you thought you were. I remember a girl in the neighborhood told my daddy to kiss her ass. Daddy chased the girl with his knife he kept on him. We had to call Momma from work. Daddy always demanded respect and by all means necessary, he got it.

***Daddy always demanded respect and by all means necessary, he got it.***

Momma had this good friend, JJ, who was a homosexual. He lived right next door to us in our first apartment, the two-bedroom. We loved him and he was remarkably close to our family.

JJ used to fall a lot due to his drinking. He would have knots on his head from the falls. Momma used to fall too when she drank. One time, she fell out of the bed and was lying on the other side. Daddy did not know she was over there.

When Momma and JJ drank, they watched out for each other. That gave me a little comfort, but it was also scary because guys used to beat JJ and take his money. I did not want anything to happen to Momma while she was with him.

One day, somebody beat JJ badly and he ended up in the hospital. He died as a result of the beating. I cried like he was part of our family, which in my heart he was.

***They watched out for each other.***

Momma had another friend she used to drink with named Smokey. I did not like her. It was just something about her. I didn't feel the closeness to her like I did JJ. He really cared about our family, and it showed.

One day, Smokey made me, and Hester get on top of her with no clothes on and she was hunching us. Momma and Daddy had left us with her. I don't know why she did it and I can't even remember how old I was. Hester wasn't in school yet, but I was. I didn't know what to feel. I knew it was wrong and she was big and fat. I was scared to tell Mama and

Daddy, but Hester was always the dare devil. She was not scared of anything. She told Momma and Daddy when they got home. I do not know why Daddy and Momma left us with her and until this day, she and Momma are still friends. I cannot stand the sight of her. I speak but nothing more, nothing less.

***"But as for you be strong and do not give up, for your work will be rewarded." 2 Chronicles 15:7 KJV***

## Daddy's Girl

I was a Daddy's girl. Momma said that when Daddy left the house and he did not take me with him, when I was a young girl, I would fall out on the floor hitting my head. I did not care. I just wanted my Daddy. I would get up in the window and wait until he came home.

We, me, and my Daddy, had a bond that was unbreakable. I don't know how it happened, but I know we had this thing. I remember sucking my finger while rubbing his elbow. I would do it just in passing or if he was lying down or if he was sitting at the table. It was just a habit. I don't know why. It is just what I did, and he allowed it. Maybe it was just our bonding time. I don't even know how it started.

The first night I got my period, Daddy was at work. When he came home, he had every size pad you could think of under his arms. I was eleven years old. He wanted to make sure that I, his Daddy's girl, didn't lack what I needed. (His baby girl is becoming a woman.) He was my protector, my hero, my make-sure-I-had-everything-I-needed-Daddy.

I am so much like my Daddy. He had these big eyes. Momma does also but mine are more like Daddy's. I looked more like Momma now but when I was younger, I looked more like Daddy. Now when I close my eyes, they don't close all the way just like daddy eyes were. I act just like him. I have a smart mouth and I don't take anything off anybody. Momma said that Daddy was in a union on his job like I am today on my job. Every time something happens in the family, they used to call Daddy. My family started calling me whenever something happened. But over the years I had to ask my family to stop calling me about everything; it was just too stressful. When I write my bills out, I sit at my table just like Daddy did and add everything up and see what I have left. It's just amazing the connection we still have even though he is not here.

My Daddy was smooth beginning with the way he dressed in the Kangol hats that matched every shirt he would wear. These shirts had Hawaiian colors and patterns on them. Daddy also had this smooth way he walked. It was the way he carried himself. A lot of admires from the women. He was very respectful, independent but not strong in build. Daddy was a slender guy and dark skinned. But his character was strong. You couldn't get away with anything with Daddy.

***Choose to see what god has***
***placed inside you to give to the world.***
***-Chrystal Evans Hurst***

Now, my Daddy was not perfect; he loved to gamble. He bet on the dogs in Shorter at the dog track, Victoryland. (Shorter is a small town in Alabama just outside of Tuskegee, AL.) He would sit at the head of the kitchen table with this little pocket notebook and would figure all the possibilities of what order the dogs could come in. Daddy won $5,000 once at Victoryland. He came home and started to count money around Momma while she was laying in the bed. You know like a scene you would see in a movie. He was so excited.

One time, I had to walk home from school. I was terrified because I had to walk under this tunnel to get home. The kids were teasing me, pulling my skirt, and pulling my hair. When I made it home, I was just crying because Daddy never came to pick me up and that had never happened before. When Momma found out, she was pissed off. Little did I know, Daddy had lost the rent money and had gone to Selma to his family to see if he could get the money back. (One thing I can say, even with Daddy's gambling, we never had anything cut off in our house.) When she saw him coming up the sidewalk, she told me to hide. When he walked in, she asked him, "Where my baby is?" They got to fussing and cussing. I ran out and grabbed Daddy's leg while I was crying. She told him he better never leave me like that again. I am my Daddy's girl.

I remember Daddy sitting at the table crying. This was one of the first time I ever saw my daddy cry. I never saw Daddy cry before this time, and I never saw Daddy cry again after this time. This was hard for me to see. This was my daddy, a tough man. I didn't understand what would make him cry and I didn't like seeing it. One of my older sisters was on drugs and her mother called Daddy to tell him about it. I remember him saying it was nothing he could do. I think he felt hopeless. Daddy always tried to fix everything. I am the same way; I try to fix everything. The news crushed my daddy. I reminded myself of a promise to myself that I'm going after the life I prayed for...period.

***"I'm going after the life I prayed for ......period!"***

Momma always did our hair so pretty and always kept us clean. Hester and I had this exceptionally long silky black hair. Momma said that Hester and I got our hair from Daddy and Auntie, my dad's sister. Momma said when she met Daddy, he had long hair but over time with his health issues, it came out. Daddy's hair was so soft. That's all you saw under that hat. He had salt and pepper hair with a bald spot in the top. He used to tell us to get a comb and scratch all the dandruff out of the bald part of his head. Flakes would be popping everywhere but we did it.

Daddy did not want Momma to use a hot comb on our hair because he feared the heat would take it - burn it-out. However, one day, Momma did exactly that, she pressed out hair. Our hair was very long and thick, it passed our shoulders. She was pressing my hair when Daddy saw what she was doing. She and Daddy got into it about her pressing our hair. I am not sure how it happened, but I remember the hot comb ended up on my shoulder. I still have that bruise on my shoulder today. And to make things worse, Momma made me get a jerry curl in 5$^{th}$ grade, I hated it. My clothes and my pillow were always wet from it.

Daddy would always have me dial my aunt in New York's phone number. (He had everybody's number in a little pocket tablet.) Daddy was the oldest of the two siblings. Daddy and my aunt looked like twins. She had this long black beautiful hair. My aunt left Alabama in her 20s and moved to New York. She lived there until she passed away on August 25, 1995.

My aunt really helped us out a lot. My auntie could sew better than a celebrity seamstress or designer any day. She would make a lot of our Easter clothes and she always sent us our school supplies. They were always cool and different than the other kids' stuff. We would wear them no matter what they looked like. We were just grateful and liked that our clothes and supplies came from New York.

One day, Momma said, "Your Daddy is going to see his sister in New York." It had been several years since Daddy and Auntie had seen each other. I did not know how far New York was from Alabama but I did not want my Daddy to go. It felt like Daddy was gone a long time. He rode the bus up there. My auntie had eight children. My cousins surprised her with my dad's visit because it had been so long since she and her brother had seen each other; it was only the two of them. I was so happy when he got back home.

***My auntie could sew better than a celebrity seamstress or designer any day.***

Well, I am 6 years old and baby number four is here. She was bright. I thought she was white. When we went to pick Momma up from the hospital, I said, "She look white, Momma." Momma slapped me so hard I fell back in the seat. I didn't say anything else that night.

Momma was the disciplinary in the house even though Daddy didn't like for her to whip us. When she did, Daddy wasn't home. I hated going get my own switch off the bush outside. I would always come back with a little one. I hated getting a whipping with a belt, too. But I hated the switch more because it left welts on me sometimes; it even pierced the skin. Hester and Red got more whippings than Gracey and me. I wasn't a bad child. I can count on one hand, the number of times I got a whipping.

***Momma was the disciplinary in the house even though Daddy didn't like for her to whip us.***

Momma had my two younger sisters (babies three and four), Gracey and Red, so close together that it made her sick. I was later told that she had a nervous breakdown. When it happened, we went over across the sidewalk to this lady's house that Momma and Daddy knew while Daddy went to the hospital with Momma. I saw the ambulance people taking my Momma out of the house on a gurney. I was scared, and I was crying. I didn't know what was happening to my Momma. (I don't remember how long Momma was gone to the hospital, but it was a long time and when she came home, she had a prescription for nerve medicine.) While Momma was in the hospital, Daddy had to take care of us girls. He tried his best at combing our hair while Momma was in the hospital. However, my Aunt Blacky (one of my Momma's sisters) was always around. She helped a lot when Daddy or Momma was in the hospital. (Momma was not sick often. She mostly went to the hospital to have my sisters.)

Now, it's four girls in one room. We had double bunk beds. Momma and Daddy decided to move us across the street to a three-bedroom apartment. The bunk beds we had stacked in the two-bedroom, we took down in the three-bedroom. We still lived in the projects, but this was a nice change because it gave us more room. Gracey and Red had the first room when you walked into the apartment. Hester and I had the middle room and Momma, and Daddy were on the back side of the apartment.

On Saturday mornings, Junior's Daddy, and the man next door to him would get under the tree and play blues. Of course, that was the day to clean up and hang out the clothes on the clothesline. Those clothes would get so hard and stiff. I didn't like when it rained, and we had to go out and get them if they were still wet. We would have to hang them around the house to dry. It was funny when the Jehovah's Witnesses would come. Momma and Daddy would tell us to tell them they were not there, and my Momma would tell my sisters they had better be quiet.

On Sundays, Momma would get us dressed and Daddy would drop us off at church. We never went to church as a family. I used to feel sad because everyone else's family would go to church with them and most of the time, I had some skit I had to do, and they never got to see me do it especially for Easter. Church would last all day, it seemed, and do not let it be a program, it would last all day. We knew that Mom and Dad loved us even though we were never told as children; we just knew that they loved us.

***We knew that Mom and Dad loved us even though we were never told as children; we just knew that they loved us.***

## Smelling Myself

Well, its four of us now: Hester, Gracey, Red and me and we are living in our three-bedroom apartment. I am in junior high school now attending Brewbaker Junior High School. It was so far from the house—it was a 30-minute bus ride. Daddy would walk me sometimes to the bus stop in the beginning, then Momma and Daddy would just watch me from the front porch. The bus stop was not far from our apartment, and you could see the bus stop standing in our front yard. We would get up at 5am because now it is four of us trying to get ready for school with one bathroom, but we made it work.

Junior high school was a big change for me. I did not dress well nor have a lot of what the other kids had or wore. Junior high was quite different from elementary school and difficult at first. But I still had all my friends from the neighborhood and from elementary school. I was losing my protection with growing up; Daddy was not there to protect me at school or on the bus. I used to get joked on— I still had no breasts, still no butt and on top of that, I had a wet curl, and I didn't have the clothes and shoes the other kids had.

Brewbaker was not too bad. I met new friends and it was a much bigger school. We had schedules and lockers and different classes—a lot of them which were hard at first.

Daddy would help us all with homework. He was a very smart daddy. He had a 12$^{th}$ grade education, but he didn't complete high school. He went into the United States Air Force shortly after high school. Arithmetic was my weakest subject. Daddy would make me sit there until I got it right and he fussed until I would get it right.

Junior high was difficult because I used to bleed so heavy and cramp so bad when I had my period. This carried on well into my adulthood. I would mess up my clothes and this was so embarrassing especially when I was at school. Hester and I always had this friendly competition on grades and attendance. It was a tie with the grades but not attendance, although, we barely missed school. Momma and Daddy did not play that 'being out of school' game for no reason. You better be sick for real or else. I was always sick with something, either tonsillitis or heavy periods. I was sick every month with my period, so I did not have a choice but to miss school. One time, I passed out because I was bleeding so heavy. I hit my head on one of our bunk beds at home due to passing out.

***"I realized that it's not about what happens to us, it's how we handle it."***

Daddy is starting to go to the hospital a lot. One afternoon, he was in the bathroom taking a shower and when he came out, he hit the floor. I thought he had got too hot, but his potassium was low. Daddy had a heart condition. He had congestive heart failure. Momma said Daddy used to drink before I was born but then when he developed the heart condition, he stopped. But he and Momma smoked cigarettes. Daddy said he started smoking cigarettes at 12 years old.

Hester started screaming at me to call 911 and I just froze. I could not move. I could not do anything. I was screaming but nothing was coming out my mouth. Momma was at work, so she got a way home. (Momma does not know how to drive.)

***You may get tired,***
***But don't quit.***
***Your brightest days are still ahead.***
***-Dr. Jevonnah Ellison,***
***Maximum Potential Academy (MPA), Founder***

By 8th grade, I started to like this guy seven years my senior. His name was Junior. Daddy wanted to kill Junior. He knew we liked each other, but Daddy also knew Junior had several kids and he was much older than I was. I did not understand all that at that time. Daddy was not playing that. Daddy even told Junior's daddy to tell him to stay away from me. But it was something about Junior. When he pulled up playing his music, I would run to the window or door and watch him until he got home. He and his dad stayed four doors down from us. I was 14 the first time Junior and I tried to have sex. It was unsuccessful. We got scared and stopped. He did not even penetrate.

9th grade was bittersweet. I had made a lot of friends. A lot of my friends were going to Sidney Lanier not Robert E. Lee High School. I was going to

Lee. Lee was much closer to Riverside than Brewbaker Jr. High, but we still rode the bus. Going to high school meant leaving so many of my friends but on the other hand, I was going to high school. I was excited and scared all at the same time.

***"The only person you are destined to become is the person you decide to be."***
***Ralph Waldo Emerson***

## 16

When we would get bored, Daddy would show us how to play cards. We learned how to play spades and I always dealt the cards— me, being the oldest. It was fun especially because it was four of us. We played together well growing up. Daddy and Momma would not have it any other way. Daddy taught us how to play Go Fish and Tunk (all card games) and we also used to play Uno. We also had this other game we loved to play. We used to get the calculator and guess in what year what age we would be. It was fun.

Daddy loved fishing, especially down at the Alabama River which was in walking distance from our apartment. He would take our dog and when came back, he always had fish. I remember Daddy would get some newspaper and a fork, lay it on top of the washing machine lid and show me how to scale the fish, cut the head off and get all the black guts out of the fish. I hated when the scales would pop on me, but I loved eating fish. I would eat any fish, but I did not like it when the bones got stuck in my throat. I would eat fish without bread but after the bones would get stuck in my throat, Momma would give me bread to push the bones down my throat. Eating so much bread then could be the reason I do not care much for bread now.

***Worry looks around.***
***Sorry looks back.***
***Faith looks up.***
***-Margaret 'Shug' Avery, Actress and Singer***

I was 16 when I finally did have sex. It hurt. It was painful and I started to bleed. I did not like it. (I was 18 when I finally had sex again.) It happened one day when Daddy went to go get Momma from work. I sneaked down to Junior's daddy's apartment, and we had sex on his bed.

Hester knew what had happened. She told Momma and she told Daddy. (She had been trying to tell on me all day.) Daddy was so hurt and disappointed in me. I felt ashamed and felt like I broke my daddy's heart, and I did not want my daddy to get in any trouble because he really wanted to hurt Junior, possibly kill him. I was so disappointed with myself. I went in the bathroom with scissors and tried to cut my wrist. I could not go through with it, though. I just scrapped my wrist. I did not want to leave my daddy and I did not want him crying over me. (It hurt me too much to see my daddy cry.) I pulled myself together and promised myself I would never hurt my daddy again. I had that shame over my head a long time. I could sense the jealousy from Hester because of the relationship that Daddy and I had. When she told on me, that is when things changed between Hester and me.

In the 9th grade, I had two friends that was half-sisters. One of the sisters wanted Junior. (Junior and I were never in a relationship but there was something there.) They slept together and she got pregnant. I was so crushed, but it was okay because I was not loose like that, and it was for the best. (When I say loose, I say it because that was not her first-time having sex with a guy.) I knew I didn't want to be a teen mom and I knew for a fact; Daddy would have killed him if I would have gotten pregnant. I also knew I wanted to get out the projects and make a life for myself. He, Junior, kept saying "I did not know you and she was friends." I was never friends with her again.

***I pulled myself together and promised myself I would never hurt my daddy again.***

I remember Daddy used to come home with the heart monitor around his neck and the hospital would have to send the ambulance to come get it. Daddy hated to leave his family even if he was sick. Daddy used to say he would pull his hat over his eyes and walk "sneak" out the hospital. When we looked up, he would be coming through the door at our home wearing his heart monitor and all. He would say they (the doctors and hospital staff) are not going to use me as guinea pig.

10th grade was different. I gained some friends and lost some friends to other schools. Of course, I still got joked on. I still had a curl, still no breasts and still no butt and I was still not dressing like the other kids. Sometimes, I would just lay my head into my folded arms on the seat on the school bus so no one would notice me. I wanted to melt away.

***"For we are God's Masterpiece."***
***Ephesians 2:10 NLT***

I did not have a boyfriend. I was fine with that. Daddy was not playing that anyway. When guys would come by to see me, the front porch is the farthest they could come, and Daddy would be coming to the door to check to make sure you are not too close to me or trying to touch or kiss me. By now, it's starting to not be fun, and a little rebellion is coming out, but I wasn't crazy enough to try Daddy about it. I would mumble under my breath every now and again. The farthest we would go from our apartment was to the candy lady's house two rows over from us. She sold frozens, pickles, pickled pig feet, ice cream cones, etc. Those were the good days, especially in the summer when it was hot.

I remember my mom's sisters coming over one time and they all stayed outside talking. I was watching from the window. It was strange—all of them coming over like that but not coming in the house. (I don't remember how many came but there were 12 siblings, nine girls and three boys and a lot of the sisters were at our house that day.) But I knew Daddy was getting sicker.

***But I knew Daddy was getting sicker.***

On Tuesday, August 25, 1992, the day before I started the 11th grade, Daddy was sick. He could barely walk so Momma called the ambulance. They came and took Daddy out on the gurney. When he looked at me, I said, "Daddy, I promise I will take care of the family always." Before this time, we used to talk about what I was going to do when I finished high school. I told him I was going to follow in his footsteps and go in the United States Air Force like him. I knew college was not for me.

I was able to stay at home by myself with my sisters, I was almost 17. Momma had been gone all day. So, it's a little after 5 that afternoon and my Aunt Blacky came over. I was wondering why because Momma was not there but shortly after, Momma came. I noticed she stumbled when she came up on the porch, but she was not drinking. They called us in the living room and asked us to sit down because Momma had something to tell us. She said, "Your daddy died this evening."

I lost it. I started screaming and hollering. I could not believe what I was hearing. This could not be real. I just did not want to be here if Daddy was not here; I cannot do this without him. I did not get to say bye. I did not get to say, "Daddy, I love you" ...so, you mean to tell me this was the last time I was going to see my daddy. I just went and laid on his side of the bed. I cried myself to sleep. I could smell his scent. I felt close to him that way. I just wanted my daddy.

Everything is very vague to me, and it is the day before school starts. This was supposed to be a very exciting day in my life, but this was the worse day of my life. I would lay there until Momma came in the room drunk. Her drinking had gotten worse; she would drink more than she ate. I had to call my aunt and tell her Daddy was gone. That is hard on a child, but I had to do it. (Believe it or not, Daddy and my aunt died on the exact same day just three years a part. He died in 1992 and she died in 1995; both on August 25th. She is buried in Selma, Alabama.)

***"For whether we live, we live unto the Lord; and whether we die, we die unto the Lord: whether we live therefore, or die, we are the Lord's."***
***Romans 14:8 KJV***

My cousin worked at a funeral home in Selma. Momma said he was on his way to get Daddy's body. We did not have any insurance on Daddy. We buried him at the cemetery at the church he went to as a child. It is a family burial ground in Browns, Alabama. It felt like forever getting there from Montgomery to Browns, Alabama. I felt like I was in the clouds just floating. I was so numb and did not understand why my daddy was taken from me. Momma and Daddy always said do not question God, but I was so angry with God. I did not understand how He could take my daddy from me.

Daddy had an open casket funeral. My cousin cut his hair just like he wore it. He looked so handsome in his suit my cousin picked out. I remember some people who were there at the funeral. I remember my first cousin singing. But I do not remember anything else. When they closed that casket on my daddy, I could not bear it. Half of my soul and my heart were buried that day.

One of my older sisters, Lisa, didn't even come to the funeral. I hated her for years. One because she made my daddy cry because of her drug use and then, two, not to show up for his funeral. I didn't want anything to do with her.

Daddy was 62. He would have been 63 that December. Our birthdays are in the same month. I do not even remember my birthday that year. The pain I was experiencing, I cannot even describe at 16. I just know it was unbearable.

Now, it makes sense to me when a few months earlier, Momma's sisters came over and they were standing outside and would not come inside. Momma said the doctors had told her there was nothing else they could do for Daddy. He had gone into the hospital that day to have a heart catherization but because he had too much blockage, they could not do it.

***"For I know the thoughts that I think toward you, saith the Lord, thoughts of peace, and not evil, to give you an expected end."***
***-Jeremiah 29:11 KJV***

## Face To Face

Little did I know, I was in for an experience I had never came face-to-face with before. Because of Momma's drinking, I heard the family kept saying my sisters and I could get split up and that my godmother would get me. They would have to bury me next to Daddy before that happened. So, I grew up real fast. I did not have time to grieve. I had to put my feelings aside and stop crying. I had to do what I needed to do to keep us together and help Momma because of the drinking and I needed to finish school so I can make a life for me and my family and get us out of these projects. That was lot on my shoulders at 16. We started going to AA meetings. There was a lot of anger there. I blamed Momma a lot for Daddy getting worse in the hospital right before the last time he went in the hospital.

So...Daddy was in the hospital the time before the last time. He called and asked where Momma was. I knew where she was, but I did not want to tell Daddy because I did not want him to worry; he did not want us alone. When I finally told him, a few hours later, the hospital called. They said we needed to get to the hospital. Daddy had got bad, and they put Daddy in ICU. I knew what happened. He was worried about us. My anger for her, my momma, was just bad. My respect for her was gone. I blamed her for my daddy getting worse and I also carried that guilt for many years—thinking that I was responsible as well.

***"My pain is divinely connected."***

I came home from school and Momma told me, which she really did not want to, that our dog had passed away. This happened in April 1993. That made my pain worse. First, my daddy, now my dog. We had him since Hester was 3 years old. We think he died from a broken heart. That was another blow for me, and it was hard.

Lisa finally showed up. I was around at my friend's house getting my hair done. (Momma reversed my curl. I was so happy.) I got the call that she was in town, and she was at our house. I had nothing for her. I did not even want to hear her voice. I told them I did not have a sister named Lisa. How do you not show up for your daddy's funeral? Girl, bye. I have nothing for you.

I signed up for Air Force Junior ROTC going into the $11^{th}$ grade. I am a little nervous but a little excited. I only have two more years in school.

The $11^{th}$ grade school year was a very emotional year. Strange enough, I met a guy. He was in the 12th grade and was very handsome. We started talking. Alex and I fell in love. He came at the right time. I was 18 when I had sex again. Alex was the second person I had sex with. I felt like Alex and I were soulmates.

God knew what I needed. But his mom didn't like me because I lived in the projects. I heard her talking about me bad one day when we were on the phone, and I told my mom. His mom thought all females that grew up in the projects were fast and had babies and they weren't going to be anything in life. I loved his family, especially his grandmother. Alex and I had planned to join the Air Force, which we did even though he graduated a year before me. When he left and went off to basic training, I felt like I did when Daddy died. I felt like my heart and soul had been ripped out of my body again. But his mom and I grew awfully close after he left.

I think after Daddy passed; God started to mold me into the woman I am today. Strong, independent—a leader. I really missed Alex going into my senior year and Hester is pregnant. I know Daddy is not happy. We were not raised like this. He's probably turning in his grave. Momma said she used to see Daddy's spirit walking on the floor on his side of the bed. I haven't seen him but sometimes I wish I could just to say bye and tell him I love him one last time.

Now because Daddy was getting SSI and social security checks, when I turned 18, I started to get my check in my own name. Well, Momma didn't like that. She wanted me to give her my check, but I had senior expenses and I had no one to help me pay for any of it. One day, she asked me for the check, and I said no. I was washing clothes. There was a floor full of dirty clothes. She beat me with a wire hanger, and I fell in the clothes. Even until this day, I do not have wire hangers in my house.

***"Your life does not get better by chance,***
***it gets better by change."***
***-Jim Rohn***

After Daddy died, I knew I had to get away from the projects and away from Montgomery. I knew I wanted more for myself. I promised myself I would not depend on a man like my mom did my dad.

Momma didn't even know how to pay bills. Daddy would sit at the head of the table, and he kept this pocket-sized notebook in the top pocket of his shirt. He would write down all the bills and how much he would have left over. I do my bills the same way. I write them out and see what I have left over.

I didn't go to prom my senior year. I did not have a date because Alex was in the military. I knew I was going to the United States Air Force, but I couldn't score high enough on ASVAB test. (You have to score high enough on this test to enter into the military.) I was so desperate to leave, I took the ASVAB with an Army recruiter. (The score I needed on the ASVAB was different for the Army than the Air Force.) I scored a 55. Prior to me taking the test, the Army recruiter would come get me and take me to study for the test so I could make high enough to go in the military.

The day came in July 1994 for the test. The recruiter came, picked me up and the testing room was packed. After the test, I helped clean up and he was to take me home. He started to cut the lights off and he tried to kiss me. I pushed him away and then. he started grabbing my breasts. I pushed him away and I said stop. He grabbed me between my legs, and I said stop. He tried to unzip my shorts I had on, and I told him my period was on. That is the only thing that stopped him. I was so scared and ready to go home. He took me home but by the time I got home, I had messed up my clothes. (I used to bleed so heavy.)

A few months later, Momma found us a house in Ridgecrest. It was a three-bedroom, one-bath. It was hard at first because I didn't know anyone. All my friends were gone to the military or college. My sisters were going to a different school.

I never saw the Army recruiter again, thank God. But the Army didn't want to release me. I was supposed to leave for Fort Leonard Wood, Missouri on October 3, 1994. My aunt, my mom's oldest sister, made some calls. On December 8,1994, I was in San Antonio, Texas in the United States Air Force. I left a week before my 19th birthday. My family didn't even see me off. Alex's mom met me at the airport. It was bittersweet.

This, joining the Air Force, is where my heart was, and it is a promise I promised Daddy. It has been two years now since Daddy died but it feels like yesterday.

I got hurt in the military and that was a devasting loss for me. I had no intentions of going back home. When I called my mom and told her I was coming home, I couldn't talk because I was crying so hard. On the upside, I came home with my benefits. But there was no amount of money that could fill what I was feeling. So now, what do I do? School has never been what I wanted to do. My heart and soul were the United States Air Force. Alex and I had plans of getting married and getting stationed together—all of that fell apart.

***"Only Jesus Can Turn***
***A mess into a message.***
***A Test into a Testimony.***
***A Trial into a Triumph.***
***A Victim into a Victory."***
***-GodVine.com***

## Why God Me but Why Not Me

I used to ask God why he took my daddy from me but as I grew older, it got better. I would have good years and really bad years. Daddy's death anniversary and his birthday months are hard for me and sometimes those dates come and go. I just wanted to cry and sleep the pain away. I keep asking God what my purpose was and why am I here.

***"I have heard thy prayer; I have seen thy tears; behold I will heal thee."***
***2 Kings 20:5 KJV***

Eventually, Alex got married and I met this guy named William. He was cute and had a little thug in him. He stayed in and out of jail. He also smoked weed. (I never had a desire to smoke anything.) We were together for five years. There was a lot with our relationship. I took a lot off him. There were always people at our apartment when I came from school and work. I even came home one day from school and William and some girl were walking out the bathroom and he was zipping up his pants and this heifer stayed in my building. I stayed with him even after all this. Yes, I went back to school full-time. My VA check paid my rent. He worked but his income was not enough to pay all the bills.

Keke and Mimi, my friends since Head Start, ended up stationed at Maxwell Air Force Base and they got an apartment in walking distance from mine. We used to party Thursday, Friday, and Saturday. We would go to church on Sunday where their uncle was the preacher and their cousin (his daughter), Cee Cee, attended church there also. After church, we would come home and party some more (and Cee Cee was right there with us too). Those were the days. We were in our 20's.

Three years later when the lease was up, William and I moved in with my momma and now her boyfriend is staying there. William has gotten us a dog and she's here with us now, too. One day, I am in the kitchen washing my hair in the sink and I feel a finger go through my panties and into my vagina. I turned around so fast. It was my momma's boyfriend. I told William when he got home and he said, "Baby, we have to get out of here." I told my mom, but my Aunt Blacky told me, Momma said I probably liked it. I could hear Momma on the phone with her friends and sisters talking about me and William and that was the hardest thing for me.

I graduated with my associates degree in Computer Information Science in May 1999. I worked at Post-secondary Education as an intern. It was a great experience, but I wasn't getting paid.

We moved back out into another apartment but because of finances, we were not there long, and we had a devastating lost which didn't help our relationship. This time, we were good as far as our relationship just finances hurt us bad. He cooked. He cleaned. He was a good man. He took care of me while I was on bed rest.

I remember the night I got pregnant so well. I had just picked him up from jail again. July 1999 or sometime in August, I missed my period. I was on birth control pills to help with the cramps and the length of my periods. My period was a week-long and the first day, I would get very sick to the point of vomiting from the pain. I was taking 2-3 pills 500/800 mg Motrin the VA would give me or either Goody Powder and a coke, nothing helped me. My period was so regular. I could tell the day and time it was coming on. The birth control pills made me irregular.

Now, I am pregnant. I have an appointment the first week of September. We were very excited. Our first baby. I was due April 7, 2000. I was looking for a job. He was working but he wasn't making enough, and this apartment's rent was more than my last apartment, so this is all of my disability check. The stress was bad, and we only had one car, so I walked or caught the bus most of the time. Well, I am starting to spot but I don't know why. I go to the doctor, and they put me on bed rest. This is not good. I am only nine weeks.

So, I go on bed rest. I started to cramp, still spotting and called my doctor. They said go to the

ER. I went to Jackson Hospital. While sitting at Jackson Hospital, I had this desire to push and pee. I went to the bathroom and there my baby was—all black in the toilet. I flushed and I came out crying. They called me to the back. I am still crying as they did a vaginal ultrasound. My baby is gone. They said the baby broke away from my uterus, the break was clean, and they wished I would not have flushed. They could have tested the baby to see what happened and why I miscarried. That was the hardest thing for us. (Now even with his stuff, William had some positives, too and one of those was that he could clean a house.) So, the next day, he was trying to do one of the things he did best. He was trying to clean the bathroom. It was just a routine cleaning. We both sat on the floor and cried. Our relationship was not the same after that.

In November 1999, we moved out of the apartment because we couldn't afford it. I went home and he went to his aunt's house. In February 2000, while I was visiting him, he said he didn't want me anymore. Then, a girl pulled up at his aunt's house and he got in the car with her. Shortly after that, he left Alabama, moved to Georgia, and got married sometime after that. At that time, I realized we were over. That was unbearable pain: to lose my baby and a few months later for him to leave me. We had been together for five years. It hurt me so bad. I started to lose weight. I lost 50 pounds.

I got a job at a hotel with my cousin. I was taking tests for State jobs. I was filling out applications and the only response I was getting was you are overqualified. I felt like a failure again.

***"Your transformation will make no sense to those who are not meant to be part of your next level."***
***Vibrational Revelations***

## Faith Over Fear

It's December 2000. I am 25 years old. One day, I am walking down the street and this sexy black dark like blacker-the-berry-kind-of-dark, very handsome man pulls up. He asked me my name and then, he got out of the car. We start to talk and exchange numbers. His name is Jaque. We went on our first date in March 2001. It was a good date. We went to Applebee's. He is very mature. He has been in the Marines. He has been married before and has a daughter and a son. I enjoyed our time together.

Jaque and I had been together 2 years before I started working at the Post Office. He had changed jobs as well. He started his new job a year before I started at the Post Office. I started in Tuskegee at the Post Office as a city letter carrier in July 2003.

In July 2005, I bought my home. I was very excited. I had saved up money while staying with Mom for the last 6 years. (Six years living in the same house with Mom was not always easy but it was necessary. I had a goal.) If I needed a break, I either went around to Jaque's house before he moved back in with his parents or got me a hotel room. Who would have ever thought that the big eye girl from the projects would go into the military, get a degree, buy a home, and have an amazing career? I knew as a child

I didn't want to be a statistic. I knew I was going to be somebody great.

***"The Lord himself goes before you and will be with you;***
***he will never leave you nor forsake you.***
***Do not afraid; do not be discouraged."***
***Deuteronomy 31:8 NIV***

In September 2003, my mom was in a car accident in which she was a passenger. My aunt, her oldest sister, called the Post Office in Tuskegee. My Postmaster, my boss, took me to the side and he said, "Your mom has been in an accident. I can take you to Montgomery."

I said, "Thank you but I am good. I can drive". Nothing but God got me down the road to Jackson Hospital. I don't even remember getting to the Hospital. I was numb.

I felt like a scared little girl. This is only the second time I have seen Momma in the hospital. I said, "Lord, please don't take my momma. She is all I have left". She had a broken arm, and she was diagnosed as a diabetic.

***Surely goodness and mercy shall follow***
***Me all the days of my life; and I will dwell***
***in the house of the lord forever.***
***Psalm 23:6 NIV***

In October 2003, Brady was born. He is the first grandson in the family, and we were ecstatic as a family. In August 2007, Slim is born and is the second grandson in the family. Red is their mother. When Slim was two months and Brady was four years old, Red gets caught stealing in a store while I am sitting in the car waiting for her to come out. She didn't have a car, so I took her to the store. The kids are in the store with her. I hear a tap on my window and it's a guy from the store asking me to come in the store because my sister has been caught stealing and the police are on their way. When I walk in, she is in handcuffs. Little did I know, my life was getting ready to change.

Red is taken downtown to jail and put on a County Hold. Apparently, she was wanted in Chilton County for another charge. I paid the money for the theft in Montgomery and then she was released to Chilton County. I drove to Chilton County for her hearing.

I got her an attorney that I paid for. In October 2007, Red was sentenced to six months in jail. The kids had been staying at Momma's house since Red has been locked up a few weeks. When I got back to Montgomery after the court date, I went by Momma's to tell Brady about his mom. While I'm there, Momma says, "I am not keeping any children." I was broken-hearted at that time. I said I will get them. I packed them up and went by Red's house and locked everything up. I got them more clothes and toys and I took them home with me. That was extremely hard. I didn't have a clue what I was in for, but I knew I wasn't going to allow my nephews to go into the system. I put them in daycare because I was still working in Tuskegee. I was paying Red's bills to make sure everything was kept on and checking her house every week. Well, she came home December 18, 2007, which was good.

A week after Slim turned one in September 2008, Red goes to report to her probation officer, and they lock her up for not paying restitution and the kids are with her. Momma got the kids again. We go to court in Chilton County with her attorney. I am the only one to show up out of the family. They give her 15 years. I wanted to pass out. What am I going to do with two kids for 15 years? How do I break this news to her children and my mom?

When I walked in the house, I sit the kids down and tell them. Brady said, "She told me she wasn't going to leave me again." That was heart breaking to hear.

Momma said, "You will have to get them. I can't do it."

I was so hurt but I didn't have a choice again. So, I cleaned out Red's apartment, cut everything off and moved the kids' stuff to my house. I set their room up and we became a family.

***I was so hurt but I didn't have a choice again.***

It was so hard raising two children while working in Tuskegee which is 45 minutes away from our home in Montgomery. We had to get up early. Brady attended before and after school care and he had to be picked up by 6 pm. Coming from Tuskegee some days, it was exactly 6 when I pulled up. Everyone at their school knew my situation, so they helped me so much. I put Slim in a Christian private school that was $500 a month not including his lunch which was $20.00 a week. I was sending Red money and whatever she needed while in prison. I also was making sure she could talk to the kids on the phone, and we even visited a few times but after Slim couldn't wear a pamper in there, I was done. No more visitations and I didn't want them to see her like that and in that atmosphere. Every night by 8pm, dinner had been served. We ate together. I would have Brady pray sometimes. I would pray over them as they slept. When they got in bed, I would get my Bible and read. I know it was not anybody but God that got me through these next 3 years— mentally, financially, and physically.

I had to file for temporary custody of the boys. The State gave me only $187.00 a month for them. I would buy their snacks and small personal items and pay for Brady's lunch for the month. I made too much income to qualify for free lunch. So, he had to pay for lunch which was $50.00 I paid by the month. Every week, his before/after school care was $55.00. This was a lot of money, and it was not including all my bills like the mortgage.

Over time, I bonded with Brady and Slim like they were mine. They never went without, and nothing ever got cut off. We were in church almost every Sunday. Slim was a handful so I took my belt or a ruler everywhere I went. He would crawl under the pews, hit people, etc. This was just some of the stuff that made him a handful.

One time, Slim hit Brady in the head with the cordless phone. We were just sitting on the floor watching Shrek. Then another time, Brady took Slim's face and hit it into the windowsill in their bedroom. I couldn't let that continue. They were so angry. I put them in counseling even though they were young.

I really didn't have a life much now that I had them. Jaque was still hanging in there with me despite everything going on. We have been together about eight years now. Momma would watch the boys one weekend out of the month for me and that's when Jaque and I would spend some quality time together. When we were together, I didn't have to worry about anything. I felt protected around him.

In August 2011, I get a call from Red. She was getting out of prison, and she needed a way home from Birmingham, Alabama. She was on a work release program there. (She got her own ride and didn't need me to pick her up.) I surprised the kids when I picked them up from school and we went to my mom's house which is where she was and was going to be living.

I didn't get a hug. I didn't even get a thank you and still haven't. She criticized how her kids looked and what they had on. They had on Jordans, something she could never afford. They had been in school all day. They are boys and they looked like boys who had been in school all day.

***"Be not quick in your spirit to become angry, for anger lodges in the heart of fools." Ecclesiastes 7:9 ESV***

My hell started that day. My mom was sitting there and didn't even open her mouth to defend me. Over the next few months, the verbal attacks got worse. She filed to get her children back and she was pregnant. We are sharing custody at the time. She got them on Friday evenings, every other weekend, and returned them to me on Sunday evenings, most times Hester was helping her plot against me. They talked about me all on social media.

I would take the boys to get haircuts when it was my weekend. One Friday, we are sitting in the barbershop, and I noticed Brady has bruising on his legs. He said, "Auntie, they are on my stomach too." My baby is eight years old. Nino, my sister's boyfriend, had been beating him. I called the police and reported it to the police. They referred me to Child Protect. (Child Protect is a local organization that, among other services, assists with investigating child abuse allegations.) DHR called Red and Nino down to Child Protect. They separated us all so they could get everybody's story. I could hear her cussing.

Child Protect did nothing, in my opinion. They put those kids back in that home and she stopped me from seeing them. She always dropped Slim off at my momma's house because she didn't want to deal with him. But I think it was more so that they didn't have a bond. She treated Slim very differently and still does even now.

She used my love for the boys to always ask me for money and to help pay bills. There were days they didn't have power, or gas, and one time, no running water, no toilet—the whole time, Nino was living there. She has moved so many times, I have lost count. The kids have attended almost every school in Montgomery, Alabama.

In December 2012, the baby girl that Red had (the one she was pregnant with just after her release from prison) dies in her sleep. She was three months old. Brady found her in the bed unresponsive. He was nine and Slim was five.

Over the years, my health and sanity took a hard hit due to me trying to take care of them. It was so bad that even my off days are not mine to enjoy.

Sundays and Mondays are my off days, but my momma's appointments are on Mondays, or they needed me to take them somewhere on Mondays. My Mondays were dedicated to my family and not me. My weight and health were out of control. It was too much. Everything. God, why am I here? I have a very soft heart for the children. But I am tired. God, I can't do this alone.

***"I can do all things through Christ who strengths me."***
***Philippians 4:13 KJV***

It is August 25, 2016, and my niece Karly sends me a video. (Now, Karly is Hester's oldest daughter.) The video shows Red beating Slim and he doesn't have any outer clothes on, only his underwear. The video also showed that she had Brady holding him during the beating. (The things she did and continue do to him—I don't understand how a mother can do her child like that.) I filed to bring them home with me. They came home as an emergency placement. It was so stressful and depressing seeing them in that situation, but Slim and Brady were the only ones being abused.

When they came home, I put all of us in counseling. It was so beneficial to them and me. We were doing good until the Judge decided to send them back home on December 23, 2016. (This judge was removed from the bench for six months. I'm not exactly sure of why but I'm guessing that I wasn't the only family she was doing this to.) I spent over $5,000 on attorneys just for her to send them back. I think this judge had made up in her mind she was sending them home day one. She said the video wasn't that bad.

She allowed DHR to get my sister somewhere to live and paid all her bills even though the boyfriend was living there just so she can get her kids back. (They didn't know that he was living there as well.) But nothing changed as far as the verbal abuse, physical abuse, and neglect. It got worse. She was quicker to the call the police on her black sons than she was on her boyfriend. As we all know and have seen and learned, the police and black men in American do not mix well together. The police do not care about killing your children in front of you. How do you make your sons feel when you call the police on them? Or the boyfriend calls the police on the kids and makes it seems as though they are the aggressor?

***"I have told you these things, so that in me you may have peace.***
***In this world you will have trouble.***
***But take heart! I have overcome the world."***
***John 16:33 NIV***

## His Grace

I was at a point in my life where I didn't want to live with the stress; the depression was too much. I would go to work, come home, and go to bed. I had no life. Now, my babies are back in the same situation because of Red and Nino. They only wanted them because Slim got a check every month and she got welfare for Brady. I felt after my babies left that I had tried everything. I couldn't protect them anymore and that was the worst pain.

***"And she finally gave up, dropped the fake smile as tear ran down her check and she whispered to herself, I can't do this anymore." -Relationship Rules***

I stopped going to church. My faith in God was gone. My faith in God, I lost it so many times. Times like when Daddy passed away, when I came back to Montgomery, Alabama from the military, my miscarriage, when the relationship with William ended, and the sexual assaults from various people. The child abuse my nephews went through. I didn't understand why God would let this judge keep sending them home to an abusive mother and her boyfriend. I couldn't see past my pain. That was my first sign that I was depressed. I really didn't have a significant other to help me with the pain because I had shut down and I shut people out and I told everyone I was fine and okay. (Jaque was still hanging in there with me, but I didn't know how to let him help me with the pain.)

I faked it. That's what people that are depressed do. We put on a face. We have a face for everyone but no matter what, I always smiled. I smiled through my pain. I put on that Marilyn face. The one thing I always tell people, I will be Marilyn today, tomorrow, and next year. I don't bring my problems with me no matter where I go, and I don't talk about them.

***"I hold in a lot.***
***When I'm in pain, I don't like to worry other people.***
***No matter how hard I cry,***
***Or how much somebody asks,***
***My answers will be I'm fine.***
***Even if it's not true."***
***-Relationship Rules***

## The Little Girl Is Healed

I finally got up and started going back to church. I started to get a little better.

I started to see a psychiatrist at the VA Hospital in Montgomery and started counseling around 2013. I also received counseling from the Employee Assistance Program (EAP) which is through my job. I was diagnosed with major depressive disorder.

I thought my pain, anger, and depression came from me not being able to grieve my daddy's death. But baby, that root was deeper than that. My pain, anger, and depression started much younger. In therapy, I had to break down every relationship from my mom, dad, siblings, and past boyfriends to present relationships and how they each affected me, including every lost I have been through. We started to analyze every relationship and how it affected me individually which is something I never did. It has been a journey. So much has been revealed to me through my own eyes. I prayed to God for the healing of my heart, my soul, and my spirit.

Therapy allowed me to deal with those relationships, those individuals, and those raw emotions and at times, those emotions broke me to my core. My therapist said, "Deal with the emotions but don't live in it".

***Deal with the emotions but don't live in it.***
***-Dr. S***

When I would have triggers or setbacks, I was allowing those emotions to take over me for days or control me for days. During those times, the psychiatrist told me to do some self-care—go get your nails done, have a massage, read a book, etc. I had to learn self-care because from the age of 16, I had been taking care of everyone else and not myself. I didn't know how to take care of me. I didn't know myself. I didn't love myself enough to trust that I could be at peace and love myself first. That part was very hard for me in the beginning.

After I was diagnosed with a heart condition in 2018 and a blockage in 2020, which if it gets worse will require heart surgery, I knew that I had to take better care of myself which included eating better and weight loss. I exercise three to four times a week. I meal prep and I cook my meals for the week. This keeps me from stopping at fast food chains or eating out. When I started my weight lost journey in September 2019, I was 225. Now, I weigh 205 pounds. It has not been easy, but I know where I came from, and I don't want to weigh that again.

I pray more. I am learning to mediate, just sitting still, and relaxing my mind and spirit. I had to learn self-care and self-love because I was so used to taking care of others most of my life. I don't do everything I set out to do like I used to. My attitude now: if it doesn't get done, oh well. I don't get upset like I used to. I had to tell the kids, "Auntie has to take care of me first so I can be around a little longer." I must be healthy.

Over the years, I have gotten better. My anger is so much better and surviving depression is so much better. I had to learn from the psychiatrist to live in the moment of my depression but don't allow it to hold me hostage. I have learned self-love and self-care. It's still a challenge because I have triggers, but I am so much better because I allowed God to heal me. I opened my heart and my mind to receive and to hear God's voice. I also had to forgive and honey, that's when the breakthroughs started to flow.

***"For the anger of man does not produce the righteousness of God."***
***James 1:20 ESV***

I know I am healing because the anger I used to have, I don't have anymore. I remember one time; I was in a meeting, and I said to the other female that I was sorry. Her statement was I don't know what you saying I am sorry to me for. When I left that meeting, before I knew it, I said, "If you don't get her, I am going to kill her." I knew then my anger was at its peak.

Due to the stress from everything I was going through, I developed irritable bowel syndrome (IBS) which is an intestinal disorder causing pain in the belly, gas, diarrhea, and constipation. According to information that I found on the internet, people exposed to stressful events, especially in childhood, tend to have more symptoms of IBS. The pain from IBS is very painful. I am not easily to get angry like I used to because my stress is not like it used to be. My IBS has not flared up in years. I have learned to pray and let God fight my battles because if I do not, it's not going to work out in my favor, and I will be in prison.

***"I have learned self-love and self-care***.

## The Sky Is The Limit

As mentioned earlier, I started counseling around 2013 and am still getting it to this present day. I never thought in my life I would be in therapy, seeing a psychiatrist. I am so thankful that I did and that am continuing it.

I did not think I would live to see 45 years old. I didn't know I had a purpose. I am just a young girl that grew up in the projects were getting pregnant at a young age was common and were living in poverty was normal. (I didn't know we were poor until I got older.) All I knew was that I had a lot of pain. I felt lost. I felt unwanted. There was no one to protect me from this cruel world. I was alone. As the years came and went, the pain got worse, and my purpose was very uncertain. I felt unloved. I didn't love myself. I felt unappreciated.

***"We have a pulse for a purpose."***

But at 45 that devil was a lie because God healed me. He turned my pain into my purpose. I have had breakthroughs in my family and in relationships. I forgave people that brought me so much pain mentally and physically and I took my power back. Before He healed me, I didn't have faith in God anymore. I felt like He did not love me anymore. I didn't believe I was worthy anymore. But God broke those generational curses.

I am a survivor. I am healed and I believe I have my faith back. I have my power back all because of God. I keep remembering God saying, "I will not leave you or forsake you." But I had to get where I am today to feel that, to trust that and step out on those words.

***I keep remembering God saying, "I will not leave you or forsake you".***

As I got older and with the counseling's help, I saw my situations differently. Daddy had to die for me to live and become the woman God had destined me to be—which is an independent, self-sufficient, and hard-working woman. I don't take anything off nobody. My miscarriage and my relationship with William had to end because there was no growth there—that was a dead situation. I also realize that I came home back to Alabama because I had a purpose here. I have made a difference in so many people's lives, not only my family and friends but now with my book, I will change lives around the world.

There were times I couldn't even say "Daddy" or "Eddie" before the tears would fall because of the pain and the loneliness of not having him here with me. But God! Now, I can say his name and not cry and that's how I know I am healing. It is a process. I needed to confront all my relationships and losses to get me where I am today. My life wouldn't be what it is today without the counseling and my God.

***"My help comes from the LORD..."***
***Psalm 121:2 NKJV***

My life now is just so much more bearable. My momma is 69 years old now. I know we have not had the best relationship, but I love me some Mary Goldsby. She is all I have left on this earth.

I still have episodes with my depression, but I am not where I used to be, thank God. I have triggers, mainly loneliness triggers more than anything. When I go home on Saturdays, knowing that there is no one there, it makes me depressed sometimes. I go home, play my music, and clean up or sometimes I just bathe and go to bed. I think I try to sleep my depression away. I know it's all a steppingstone, and it's work and that it takes time. But I have conquered so much of my depression. It used to take a hold of me like two dogs fighting and you can't pull them apart. Now, it's not all the time and it doesn't last for days.

***I know it's all a steppingstone, and it's work and that it takes time.***

What my nephews went through and are going through still, have made them stronger mentally and physically. Brady graduates from high school in May 2022. He will be 18 in October 2021. He was four years old when I got them the first time. He is smart and he is my all-American athlete. He has run track, played basketball, but his heart, his passion, is playing football. He has played football since elementary but the other sports he played them well with no practice.

Slim used to be so angry and had that 'I don't care attitude' and was always getting in trouble. Slim was two months old when I got them the first time. He will be 14 in August 2021. Now, Slim will start high school this year. The anger is so much better; no fighting like he used to. He is much calmer.

They are both so handsome and I love them so much. I get to see my babies play on the same team this year—that is the highlight of my life. To see that everything they have been through from abuse mentally and physically to homelessness and they are still thriving and being successful. They have not given up. They keep pushing and that, within itself, gives me motivation.

Jaque. Yes, he is still my significant other. We have been in each other's lives for 20 years. We both grew up in the projects, so we understand each other.

We also understand what it is to not have. I think what attracts me to him is his strength. He resembles my dad, and they have similar traits, too. Jaque was in the Marines Corp, so there's that discipline and respect that my dad had. He is a great father to his children, as well as a great role model for any young man. I enjoy our conversations and our time together. He keeps me grounded. He gives me strength. When we are together, I am calm. I am happy. On top of all that, he is so sexy, and he has a good heart. When I am with him, I don't have a care in the world—my anxiety is not there.

We are totally opposite, but we connect. The tone of his voice never changes unless you're talking Auburn football which he really likes. Then, he may get a little loud. I am an Alabama fan, so we always have a friendly competition. (If you know anything about the State of Alabama, you know that every resident has to choose between being an Auburn University or University of Alabama fan. It's a must. It's that serious!) My voice is not soft, but I am not loud either. He is very laid back. Not me. I'm like...ok, wait a minute. Yeah, I'm up in your face.

I love how he takes care of his family. I look at how a man treats his parents, his children, and his family. I look at the heart and see if I see God in them. If there is no God in you, I can't be in a relationship with you because I am not marrying potential. I don't want to raise nobody grown at 45 or 46 years old.

I know that God will not leave me or forsake me. Everything works out just like He wants it. Yes, we go through stuff, but I won't let the situations take over my life again. Because more so, now than ever, I know where my help comes from. All I must do is put my armor on and be ready. God is fighting my battles. My armor is my anointing, and He is not going to let anything touch me that He can't fix.

At night when I pray after I tell God thank you, I ask Him to keep me on the path He has designed just for me. I ask Him to prepare me to walk in my destiny and paths that are curvy, make them straight. I also ask Him to prepare to be a wife to the man He has just for me. But most of all I ask Him to allow me to know His voice over other voices and spirits.

***"For we live by faith, not by sight."***
***2 Corinthians 5:7 NIV***

## Conclusion

We have come to the end of my first published book but certainly not the end of my story. I want to encourage you that regardless of what you have experienced, witnessed, or endured; life is not over for you either. Just like God healed me, He can and will do the same for you.

My story involves verbal abuse, physical assault, loss, betrayal, and molestation. Yours may be like mine or altogether different. However, our God is the same and what He does for one of us, He can do for any of us.

I encourage you to be open to participating with professional help if it is what you need. Getting professional help does not make you weak, it actually shows how strong you are. It shows that you are strong enough to know you need help and then have the courage to go get it. Look at it like this: If a bone was broken in your body and causing extreme pain, wouldn't you go to seek professional medical help? People would think something is wrong with you if you continued to be in pain because of a broken bone but you did not get the professional help needed. As a matter of fact, if we don't seek the professional in a timely manner, the bone will heal on its own but maybe not correctly and it may affect future use of the body part connected to the bone. Well, our internal brokenness is no different.

I hope that my sharing my story inspires you to get what you need so that you can move to the next level. I hope that my story shows you that no matter what it looks like on the outside, everybody has or is overcoming something.

**Be blessed and stay encouraged.**

## *More From the Author*

## Questions For the Author

1. What led you to write your book, *When the Little Girl is Healed, The Woman Will Show Up*? I have a friend that wrote a book on domestic violence. I read her book in one day and it was self- published. I saw her healing and I realized if God could heal her maybe He can heal me. I was tired of being depressed, angry and crying all the time.

2. Why did you choose that title, *When the Little Girl is Healed, The Woman Will Show Up*? I saw it somewhere and it spoke to my spirit, and I said, "Marilyn, that's it."

3. How long did it take you to start noticing healing? As I started to write, the pain got worse at first because I was living everything over again by remembering and a lot of it, I had suppressed. Then I started to have revelations about events that happened in my life. My mom was one of the reasons I was so angry.

4. Why therapy and not church? My faith was not strong enough to just rely on God, so I needed professional help. With the two together, it helped me a lot. I also started to fast for a

week, once a month. Slowly my faith got stronger. Something to remember is that healing doesn't have to happen because of therapy or church. It can be, and if we are honest with ourselves, it should be both.

5. Did you want to give up on life? Yes, I did, so many times. At one time, I didn't even care if I woke up or not. In my younger days, I attempted to take my life, but I couldn't stand the pain I was going to put my dad through.

6. Why didn't you give up on life? God didn't let me. I always knew I was different, but I didn't realize until now how much of an impact I can have on somebody's life through my testimonies and healing.

7. Why did you put on a fake face all those years? I am a very private person and being the oldest and put in an adult position at 16, matured me before my time. I was always told to be strong, and I taught myself to be independent and hide my feelings. I didn't want the sympathy.

8. How did your family feel after telling them about your book and what happened to you? My mom and my sister were proud of the book but also confused on why I never told them about my depression and the sexual assaults.

9. Are you happy now? How do you feel? I am happier and I am at peace, but it took me 20 plus years to get here. I keep thinking, I went through all that for what's happening right now: HEALING and releasing.

10. Why did you never tell anyone? I didn't want to be judged. Some of the stuff I did tell, and I was blamed, or no one believed me. So, I kept everything to myself.

11. Can I heal from my past? Yes, you can but you have to allow God and sometimes, a professional to help you. We can't do it on our own.

12. Will God forgive me? Yes, He will. I am not perfect. I have cursed people out. I have been cheated on and I have cheated. I have done things that only God knows about that I am not proud of. But I don't beat myself up for it. I just do better because I know better. At the end of the day, God forgives us of our sins daily, but we must repent and ask for forgiveness, peace and understanding.

13. What is depression? It is a mood disorder that causes a persistent feeling of sadness and loss of interest according to the Mayo Clinic. I was like this for several years before I was diagnosed with major depressive disorder which is clinical depression. It affects how you

feel, think, and behave and can lead to a variety of emotional and physical problems.

14. What is anger? A strong feeling of being upset or annoyed because of something wrong or bad; the feeling that makes someone want to hurt other people, to shout (Merriam-Webster Dictionary). I kept a lot of my anger internal but when I released my anger, it was bad.

15. What is sexual assault? It is an act in which one intentionally sexually touches another person without that person's consent or coerces or physically forces a person to engage in sexual act against their will (rainn.org). When the Army Recruiter tried to have sex with me, when my mom's boyfriend stuck his finger in my vagina, when my friend's husband sexually harassed me and then tried to physically restrain me to the point I had marks on my body, those are examples of sexual assault acts. (I do not talk about the last experience in this book.)

16. What is molestation? To make unwanted or improper sexual advances towards someone specially to force physical and sexual contact on someone (Merriam-Webster). When my mom's friend made me get naked and she touched me and made me touch her is an example of molestation.

17. What is the meaning of parent/child role reversal? When the parent looks to the child for nurture, protection and affirmation, and the child, either consciously or unconsciously sacrifices his or her needs to provide for the needs of the parent (Hometownsource.com). I remember when my daddy died. That day, even though I had just lost my dad, I had to call my aunt and tell her that her brother had passed. I had to pay bills for my mom because she didn't know how to budget and pay bills. I took care of my sisters when Mom was in the streets drinking.

18. What is the meaning of neglect? It is frequently defined as the failure of a parent, or other person with responsibility for the child to provide needed food, clothing, shelter, medical care, or supervision to the degree that the child's health, safety, and well-being are threatened with harm (Childwelfare.gov). The older guy I feel in love with at 16 or 17 was due to lack of love for myself. It was neglect because I didn't have anyone supervising me. I started to act out by being sneaky and having sex at an early age.

19. What is alcoholism? A chronic disease characterized by uncontrolled drinking and preoccupation with alcohol (Mayo Clinic). As of 2021, my mom has been sober for three years. Thank you, God. It is such a blessing and her walk and faith with God is even stronger. She

even prays for me and tells me she loves me now. All my life, my mom has always drunk, and it got really bad when Daddy passed away. She became abusive—verbally, emotionally, and physically.

20. What is the meaning of losses? The fact or process of losing something or someone (Lexico). I lost my daddy, my baby, my five-year relationship. I even lost my will to live.

21. How do people see you after hearing your story? So many people didn't have an idea I had been through even a portion of what I am sharing. So many are still very shocked and sympathetic. But so many are so proud because of my healing and how what I have survived can help heal so many more.

22. What do you expect from people hearing your story and reading your book? Healing, peace, and breakthroughs. Forgiveness is not for the other person. Forgiving is all about you. It's okay and very important to forgive yourself when you need to My hurt was not my fault and I forgave the other person internally because I was giving them too much power with the anger and the hate. I had to release it in order for God to heal me. God stripped me down to my bare soul and rebuilt me with faith and purpose. He was putting me on my path of what I was destined to do.

23. How's your faith? How did I get my faith back? With fasting, praying and crying a lot on my knees to God asking why I am here, what is my purpose. I say a prayer at night that says, "Prepare me to be the woman you have destined me to be. Any road that is not Your path, make it straight so I can do Your will". I would ask God to heal me spiritually, physically, and mentally. Then I would take my hand, put it over my heart and say, "God, heal my heart." I noticed God started to remove people from my life and I was fine with it. I didn't ask any questions. Situations that I stressed about; He gave me clarity. But most of all, I had peace. (I used to be so cold-hearted, which was coming from what I had been through.) My shoulders didn't feel heavy anymore. God had to build me up to trust only Him.

24. How's your relationship with God now? I pray more. When I speak, God comes out. The anointing in me is coming out more and more.

25. How do you to free yourself from the guilt and shame? Forgive yourself; forgive your perpetrator, the person who hurt you. Allow God to take you down to the bare nothing but you have to open your heart and trust Him. Prayer and fasting, talking to someone you trust and telling your story, you can help heal somebody. Everyone has a story.

26. How do you get your power back? I stopped fighting against what God was doing in my life. I just got tired and let it go and that is when the changes and healing started in my life. My peace and understanding came; less anger and more love came from me. Everything I had been through actually made me stronger spiritually, mentally, and physically.

***"If you believe, you will receive whatever you ask for in prayer."***
***Matthew 21:22 NIV***

## About The Author

Marilyn Evans is a daughter, sister, aunt, and friend. Her nieces, nephews and her god children motivate her to be the best she can be.

She graduated from Robert E. Lee High School in Montgomery, Alabama in 1994 and graduated college in 1999 with an associate degree in Computer Information Science. She is also a United States Air Force Veteran. She has worked for the United States Postal Service as a City Letter Carrier for 18 years.

Her healing doesn't have a look, it is not magical or pretty. Her healing was hard and exhausting. She encourages others to allow themselves to go through it and thank God at the same time.


You can follow the author at:

Instagram: Marilyn.Evans1

Twitter: @Marilyn5925

Facebook: Marilyn Evans

Email: Marilyn.evans29@yahoo.com

Website: www.marilynevansenterprises.com

## Resources

A huge part of why I wrote this book was to help others. There is no shame in asking for help. Here are some resources that I hope will be helpful to you.

<u>Addictions</u>

Alcohol Addiction 1-800-854-6025

Mental Health Hotline Banyan Treatment Centers

1-888-376-1648

<u>Child Abuse</u>

Childhelp National Child Abuse Hotline

1-800-422-4453

Ena Friday, Child Sexual Abuse Advocate and Author

www.EnaNichelle.com

<u>Domestic Violence</u>

Domestic Abuse Hotline Violence

1-800-799-7233

Tajana Bagley, Domestic Violence Advocate and Author
Amazon.com: A Girl You Know: A Survivor's Memoir; How to escape, understand and recover from abuse. (9781792317446): Bagley, Tajana Y, Huber, Krista: Books

Sexual Assault
RAINN (Rape, Abuse & Incest National Network)
800-656-HOPE (4673)
www.rainn.org

Suicide
National Suicide Prevention Lifeline
1-800-273-8255

# References

Ralph Waldo Emerson. www.quotefancy.com

Jim Rohn. www.yourtango.com; www.buiness.com

Vibrational Revelations. www.Quotesgram.com

Relationship Rules. www.relrules.com

"depression". www.mayoclinic.com

"anger". www.merriam-webster.com

"sexual assault". www.rainn.org

"molestation ". www.merriam-webster.com

"parent/child role reversal". www.hometownsource.com

"neglect". www.childwelfare.gov

"alcoholism". www.mayoclinic.com

"losses". www.lexico.com